LESSONS
and
REFLECTIONS

LESSONS
and
REFLECTIONS

Debbie Haskins

XULON PRESS

Xulon Press
2301 Lucien Way #415
Maitland, FL 32751
407.339.4217
www.xulonpress.com

Printed in the United States of America.

Paperback ISBN-13: 978-1-66281-114-2
Hardcover ISBN-13: 978-1-66281-115-9
Ebook ISBN-13: 978-1-66281-116-6

DEDICATION

This book is dedicated To my family.
Many of the lessons we learn are from our families and this book
wouldn't be complete without the lessons I have learned from you.

TABLE OF CONTENTS

Acknowledgements

Thank you to the staff at Xulon Press who guided me through writing and production Process.

Thank you to my Mom and friends, Cheri Livoti & Kim Hutchinson, for being my preview team providing valuable editing comments and suggestions.

INTRODUCTION

GREECE, NEW YORK, has always been my hometown. I had previously lived right down the road from Greece Volunteer Ambulance for ten years, and I walked past it on my way home from school. In the 1970s, *Emergency* was my favorite TV show. I knew early on that I wanted to be an Emergency Medical Technician (EMT).

I met my friend Heidi when I was sixteen, and when I learned she was a member of the Greece Volunteer Ambulance Explorer Post, I wanted to join immediately. As a teenage volunteer, I learned more than first aid skills. I learned how to work as a team with people who had been EMTs, police officers, and firefighters for years. I discovered what it took to earn the respect of those very people. I developed compassion, empathy for patients and their families, and the perseverance and adaptability required when situations and equipment did not work as planned.

I earned my certification as an EMT when I was eighteen years old and recertified three more times for a total of twelve years. The rewards of volunteering are still present in my everyday life. I have very dear friendships that have endured for over thirty years.

After I married my husband Mike, and our sons Ben and Chris were born, I redirected my volunteer efforts to our church, Bethany Presbyterian Church. As our sons became old enough to join the Boy Scouts, my volunteer work expanded as an Assistant Den Leader, Assistant Scoutmaster, and Merit Badge Counselor. I am very proud to say that both Ben and Chris earned their Eagle rank.

I decided to return to college in 2010. After finishing up courses at Monroe Community College with an Associate's Degree in Liberal Arts, I dove headfirst into the Emergency Management program at Empire State College. I finally earned my Bachelor of Science in Community and Human Services, with a concentration in Emergency Management, in 2013. I have no doubt that earning this degree opened new career opportunities that were not previously available. I have faith that God has a plan for me that best utilizes the passion He created in me to help others in emergency situations.

1

FAMILY

FAMILY MEANS MANY different things to many different people. For me it was my parents and siblings when I was growing up. I was also blessed to have my extended family of aunts, uncles, cousins, and grandparents close by. When I married Mike, "family" grew to include his parents, siblings, and nieces and nephews.

As the oldest of my siblings, I have always been very conscientious about not being bossy or overbearing; I am careful to respect my family members' decisions and privacy. I think the hardest part of being a family is respecting personal space, and acknowledging the fact that each member is their own person. It is also difficult to accept that we don't have to know everything that is going on, and that we need to give each other space and time to share when ready.

My parents have always been great examples of the kind of person I wanted to become. They have had successful businesses, including my dad's work in construction and restoring antique and custom cars his entire adult life. When he wasn't working or in his shop, he was out in the yard, mowing, cutting firewood, or cleaning the pool. He taught all three of us how to do them all.

Mom owned her own fitness business for several years, all while managing three teenagers, doing all the cooking, cleaning, and laundry. She always made our home warm and welcoming for us and all who entered.

Together, they restored an old house, which my sister lived in for a while, and then turned it into a country gift store. In 1991 they bought a huge old farmhouse that needed extensive work. The property included several barns and a small house. Both houses were restored, along with portions of the barns to create space for my dad to work on cars.

In 1994, they turned their home into a Bed and Breakfast which they ran for almost twenty years. During all those years, they always made time to share with friends and family.

I share this with you because it is proof of what can come from great teamwork as a couple. Their energy was contagious, and I have always admired them for that.

My sister Melanie is a paralegal. She is also a wife, and a mom to three daughters. We don't spend as much time together as we would like, but we always enjoy each other's company, and she is my cheerleader when I try anything new (like writing this book). Melanie is a runner; she even completed a half-triathlon a couple of years ago. That is so beyond my preferred level of exercise but I am very proud of her for it.

My brother, Corey, has followed my parents' entrepreneurial spirit and has owned his own home theater business for several years. I am so proud of him. Even though he is younger than I am, I look up to him for so many things. He demonstrates the same values that my parents instilled in all of us, and we all know we can always rely on him when we need him. He is always willing to share his expertise without making people feel foolish for asking.

I am still blessed to have my Family living so close. This includes my Aunt Carolyn. For over 30 years, she hosted a pre-Christmas dinner for family ranging from 15-22 people. She and Mom would collaborate on the food and it was always delicious.

Aunt Carolyn would also make trays of cookies for us all. The first few years, we would "fight" over who got which cookie, so she surprised us one year, many moons ago, with a cookie tray for each family to take home. Even though we didn't gather this year, she still took the time to make the cookies for all of us.

She has always been a very important part of my life, and I am so glad that we have been able to share such important times and turn them into memories together.

I mentioned earlier that Mike's family has become mine as well. He is one of six siblings. Being part of such a large family creates many memories. I would be remiss if I didn't include my sister-in-law Kathlene (Kathy) as an inspiration for writing this book. It was during a conversation with her about the books she has written that I was drawn to write my poem "Episodes of Adversity."

Many people have "lost" family members because of misunderstandings and conflict. My prayer is that everyone has a support network that they call *family*, whether it be through church, the military, work, volunteer services, or friendship.

For those who are separated from family because of a miscommunication, I urge you to invest the time to find a way to mend the rift. Rather than list the many reasons that miscommunications occur, I prefer to focus on how to remedy the situation. There are so many rewarding possibilities with renewed relationships. We owe it to ourselves to take that first step and see where it leads.

There are some relationships that should not be restored because they weren't healthy to begin with. In those situations, you may have to leave those in the past with the understanding that they are meant to stay in the past, all while remembering any good times that were shared.

My hope for you is that your time spent with whomever you consider family be spent joyfully and in the present. Play games, sit on the porch, and talk around the table; leave the technology at the door!

2

MARRIAGE

A Road Map to Only God Knows Where

PICTURE THIS: YOU have mapped out a whole vacation including lodging, restaurants, and entertainment venues. You are on the way to go shopping at a cute little coastal pier in Rockport, MA and suddenly—the map you thought would take you there ends. Now, that is not to say there is no pier; just that you'll need to find a detour. If that isn't a metaphor for marriage, I don't know what is.

My husband Mike and I planned a driving honeymoon through the New England states. Most of the trip was planned out, but we did dip into Rhode Island and Connecticut to expand the list of states we visited. Our first stop after staying at our family cabin was to a farm where we saw baby Bengal kittens and an adorable two-day-old donkey that followed us around.

Challenge #1 - I can't forget about the llama that I thought was nuzzling up to me when he was

5

actually working on his approach to yanking out a chunk of my hair. Okay, venue one, complete; ready to move on!

Challenge # 2 came on day three on our way to Rockport, MA. Mike was driving and I was the navigator. We were very close to our destination when the map ended and there were no signs anywhere on the road to guide us. Mike asked, "Which way?" and I told him, "I don't know, the map ended." I don't know if he didn't believe me or if he thought he knew better, but I suggested I take over driving and let him navigate, so that's what we did. I then asked him which way and he replied, "I don't know... the map ended."

I replied, "You don't say." We did eventually find the pier full of shops before too long, and it was worth it. I would even go back (with a better map).

Challenge #3 came the very next day. We had much more time than originally planned, so we thought, "Why not?" and scoped out a zoo to visit. There were over a dozen school buses, so we stayed away from the kids, and when they cleared out Mike and I headed over to the petting zoo area. I started off with feeding the Billy goats and then headed over to...yes, a llama. You know what they say, "Get back on the horse," "show no fear." Things were going well, but I started to run low on feed, so I left to turn back to feed the remainder to the goats. Well, the llama didn't agree with my decision, and before I knew it, he charged me. He "ran" up behind me, put both hooves on my backside, and pushed me to the ground. The fact that I was not injured is the only thing that saved Mike, as he was laughing along with another stranger. It was time to leave.

Outside of the three challenges, the rest of the week was incredible.

I have said for many years that if you can survive a driving honeymoon, you have got a great foundation for many successful years of marriage ahead. We just celebrated twenty-six years in May. When you have those detours and the "llama moments," you need to be able to laugh at yourself and the situation; then you will know that you can continue to make new memories and reflect with a smile on the memories you've already made.

As couples, we need to set goals—daily goals, like spending time enjoying each other's company; weekly, goals such as working on a project, playing a game, or something else outside of the ordinary chores and television;

monthly goals, like a day trip to somewhere that embraces both of your interests. Mike and I both love visiting historic forts and museums, and I love my photography, so we kill two birds with one stone on our outings (no birds were harmed during the writing of this story).

Financial planning has also got to be part of a successful marriage. There are so many instances when one spouse manages all the finances and the other is in the dark. This comes to bite them when something happens to the financial planner/manager. Working together on finances takes work, especially when two people are coming from very different backgrounds or cultures. With practice, and maybe even help from a third party, things get more manageable.

I suggest dividing the larger bills, such as the mortgage and car payment, by the number of pay days within a month, setting up direct deposit in a savings or checking account, and depositing that amount each pay period. This way, you don't have to worry about "mortgage week." The money is already there. I wish I had thought of it twenty years ago.

I know that God chose Mike especially for me. He supports my interests, friendships, and my goals; (like going back to school for my Bachelor degree). He does laundry, dishes and repairs on our appliances. Anyone who has ever needed a repairman or a replacement knows how much this can cost.

We love each other unconditionally. Even when we disagree, we always say I love you before leaving for the day, going to bed at night, and before hanging up from our phone calls. He is also a great dad to Ben & Chris. He makes the time to listen and support them in those activities that interest them.

The reason that I said "only God knows" in the beginning is because He is the one who knows us and our path, even when our maps fail us.

3

MY TWO SONS

MY SON BEN was two years and two weeks old when Chris was born. We planned to have our kids two years apart, so in a world of reproductive unpredictability, this was an amazing outcome. Ben was as excited to have a baby brother as we were to have a second son. He would constantly try to get into the playpen to be with his brother. We were convinced Chris grew fast and strong just to survive Ben's exuberance.

Ben and Chris have different personalities, as most siblings do. Ben used to climb over the baby gates, forcing us to double up on them, thereby creating our own obstacle course entering the kitchen. Chris got to the point where he just pushed the gates down. Thankfully, the baby gate days were then gone.

We have been fortunate in that while there were differences, they also had similar interests, including soccer and Boy Scouts, so we weren't pulled in all different directions. Growing up, I would say they had a 90-10 relationship; ninety percent of the time they were very close, doing everything together, and the other ten percent of the time they were arguing. My husband and I did our best to let them work things out themselves.

I have often told our sons that they can be each other's best friends, and that their brotherhood is a bond that will last their whole lives. They are the ones who must choose to make that happen. I believe some of the most important jobs we have as parents are to tell them every day how much they are loved, and to support the relationships between our children. Our greatest joy has been to see our sons grow and develop a strong friendship and sibling bond.

I originally wanted four to six kids, but Mike wanted to hold at two. For us, two worked well. Even though there was a one-to-one kid-to-parent ratio, we still had scheduling challenges when Mike and I were both working on our Bachelor's degrees and had some of our evenings tied up with class while Ben and Chris needed to be picked up from sports at two different schools.

The high school years were a balance of joys and concerns at home and school. It was reassuring to know that they were goal-oriented, and it gave us hope that they would continue to thrive into their adult years.

They are now in their twenties, and each stage of parenthood brings new feelings and provides new strategies for the next stage. The hardest lesson that I am still learning is that we need to let our adult sons make their own choices and live their own lives. We are so focused on sharing the wisdom we've gained from our experiences that we don't stop to consider that they need to have their own experiences to continue growing.

I also have to remember that times have changed, especially in the job market. Parents want their children to grow up to be able to provide for themselves, and eventually a family. The reality is our adult children are staying home longer now, and only God knows when they will be ready to move on to the next stage.

I enjoy sharing the occasional meal and feeling the comfort that we are all safely sleeping under the same roof. (I am usually the last one to bed.) At least for now, I can rest in the illusion that I still have any control over this aspect of my life. I also enjoy our conversations. It is nice learning all these new facets of these people we raised.

4

PETS

(OUR EXTENDED FAMILY)

WE HAVE HAD dogs and cats, and they were all rescues of some sort. We were very busy for several years, and we didn't feel we could have devoted the time or attention that pets deserve. In 2018, Mike and I agreed that we wanted to adopt in the fall after returning from our trip to Maine. I was searching for *a* dog: over three years old and with some level of training. I applied for at least six dogs from various rescue groups and they were all adopted before we could even get to meet them.

My friend Jacki picked Miss Bea out. I was unsure because she was younger than I planned, but Jacki persevered, pointing out Miss Bea's positive traits in the photos. I contacted the organization and expressed interest in Miss Bea (whose name we later changed to Misty). During our conversation, I revealed that we had two dogs many years ago. The lady's ears perked up and confirmed, "*Dogs?* You had *two* dogs? Would you be *interested* in adopting Miss Bea's mom, Ava, also?"

I had already spoken to Mike about the possibility of getting two dogs if they were a bonded pair, and so... we ended up with two dogs, both under two years old. We have Ava (mom) and Misty (her daughter), both adopted from Arkansas. Because they were in a shelter, potty training was not established, but they did learn fairly quickly.

Sometimes I ask myself, "What was I thinking?" (Especially when I fell and broke my ankle bringing them back in to the house one week after picking them up.) But then I settle back down, knowing how rewarding is that we rescued them both, keeping mom and daughter together in their journey to their new home. I know without a doubt that my husband and I are the right family for Ava and Misty.

My lesson is this: when making choices, I need to be open to suggestions, especially from friends and family who know me best. I was so set on finding a dog that reminded me of my departed "Mandy" that I wasn't even looking for any others that would or could be the right one(s) for me.

5

FRIENDSHIP

The very best investment we can make in our lives.

I ORIGINALLY WROTE this segment over six months ago. Unfortunately, it was part of a larger file that I accidentally deleted... permanently. A mistake that will not be repeated.

I believe it was prophetic somehow, though, because I am here writing it again just days after my dear friend Jacki's sudden passing. We had been friends since the 1980s. We used to talk at least four times a week, sometimes for an hour at a time. She almost always called like clockwork between eight and ten in the evening, and without even looking at the phone Mike would say, "Hi, Jacki," and he was right almost every time.

Friendship is a true gift, but to receive, we must also give of ourselves. Even then, some people have a difficult time developing friendships. I think high school is one of the most challenging places to find true friends.

Everyone is trying to figure out who they are becoming, what they are good at, and how to fit in.

There were people I hung out and ate lunch with, but it wasn't until my junior year that I met Nancy. We were in the same English class and had lunch at the same time for two years. We also both went to a vocational school for half the day. She and I are still dear friends today, and while we only see each other a couple of times a year, we still enjoy each other's company and keep our friendship going strong.

I have discovered that there are many types of friendships, and that each one is special and no less important than the other. There are "life-long" friendships, for instance, which start in our early years of life. Usually these are neighbors or people we meet in our first years of school. Of course, they could also be siblings or cousins.

Then there are friends that grow out of common interests, such as volunteer organizations. The friends that I met through Greece Volunteer Ambulance are absolutely priceless. I was a member for ten years and resigned almost twenty years ago. My experience has shown me that it takes a certain personality and drive to volunteer in life-or-death situations. It is those experiences that create the common bonds that really help build the friendships deep and fast.

While Jacki and Deb have been my closest GVA friends, we have also maintained connections with our other group of friends to this day. Just last night, five of us got together as a sendoff for Steve, who is moving out of state. Locations don't have to matter, though; when I called everyone to let them know of Jacki's sudden passing, it was as if we were all together again. Their love and support for Jacki's daughter and me was palpable.

There are "purpose-filled" friendships. I use that term because we all have those times in our lives when we need a helping hand. These friends may start out as people working for an agency such as home care, medical, or mental health care. Because of the nature of the business, these caring individuals may become more than caregivers; they become friends, even if only for a season. The length of time that a friendship lasts, however, does not diminish its importance.

Friendships can "occur" at all times in our lives. I met my friend Kim at a craft store about five years ago now. We recognized each other from high school pictures, although we didn't know each other then. She moved to a different school before we had a chance to meet. We got to talking after finding each other and became "fast friends." She is a kind and kindred spirit, and we both wish we had met back in school. Through Kim, I have met another wonderful friend: Jan. I thoroughly enjoy the time I spend with these ladies.

Friendships can also develop through our children. My son Ben wanted to go to a friend's house at fourteen, and I told him that I wanted to at least meet the mom first. That is how I met Laurie. She is kind and caring. She is also my "adventure" friend. She and I went zip lining along Niagara Falls a few years ago, and we have another trip planned in June of 2021. Remember, there are no age limits on adventure as long as our bodies allow! Even then, there are always modifications that could be made (possibly).

Friendships made at work are priceless. Our work friends can make bad days tolerable and great days even better. They know and understand how those challenging colleagues can make things difficult. The best part is they just brighten our days and help give us a reason to keep on going in. I have been blessed with many work friends throughout my time with many different employers. While I couldn't name them all, each one was special and irreplaceable.

I must include the dear friends that my family and I have made at church where we have been members for over twenty years. They range in age from their thirties to nineties. Out closest friends are in a group called "Shepherding." For years, we met one Saturday each month to catch up with one another and our families, have picnics, and participate in service projects. It didn't matter that we were going in all directions for sports, school, and Scouts; we all made time to get together.

Unfortunately, life as we know it has interrupted our gatherings over the last year or so and we haven't been able to meet as often as we would like. It's funny; I thought that once our kids were grown and independent, we would have more time to spend together. I hope that we resume our monthly get-togethers when time and the current health situations allow. I really miss the time we spent together.

I sincerely hope that everyone has someone they can be a friend to. The benefits are endless; friends are a reflection of ourselves, or at least part of us. True friends tell it like it is (hopefully with kindness). They provide a compassionate ear when you need to talk and help you out whenever and however they can.

If you see someone who could use a friend, I would encourage you to offer to sit down and talk with them. They may appreciate your kindness and your smile. If they aren't the most welcoming, it could be their defense "mechanism" keeping them from getting hurt again. If that is the case, just say hi and go back a few times throughout the week to check on them. If there is an issue of safety, reach out to someone more equipped to help that person. It could make all the difference in the world.

6

WAKE UP CALLS

MY HUSBAND MIKE calls me every morning to wish me a good day. Those are the wake-up calls I look forward to. Then there are those more severe wake-up calls—the ones that include car accidents that could have been so much worse than they were, or diving accidents that could have resulted in a spinal cord injury instead of just a scraped-up back. I had one of those Wake-up calls this Monday morning, April 9, on the way to work. I was less than two miles from my home. It was one of those classic "I never saw her coming" accidents. Fortunately, there were no injuries in either vehicle.

My faith in God gives me the strength and insight to use these wake-up calls to guide me in new directions, and give me new energy and focus to finish my projects, change my habits, and accomplish things I never previously considered, like writing this book (which I did on Monday as I stayed safe within my home – just for the day).

***A Poem Dedicated to Our Armed Forces
and Emergency Services Personnel***

"It's Just the Way They Are Made."

*They are born with a purpose to serve
in a field that takes skills, passion, and nerve.*

*They put strangers' well-being ahead of their own.
Their families pray that they will safely return home*

*It makes no difference whether they are volunteer or paid.
At the end of the day, it's just the way they are made.*

Debbie Haskins (2018)

7

VOLUNTEERING

OUR COUNTRY IS very blessed to have so many organizations formed, led, and run by volunteers. However, with much of our time consumed by other commitments, volunteerism has been on the decline. This is first and foremost apparent among first responders.

Fire departments and ambulance bases that had once been driven by volunteers have slowly been replaced almost entirely by paid personnel. While I was involved from 1984-1994, there was a balance between paid staff and volunteers in the larger fire departments, and GVA was entirely volunteer-based. Through the years, the fire departments have had a noticeable decline in volunteers, and now most of the volunteer ambulance bases have been bought by a larger first responder company.

At one time, these buildings were more than places to volunteer. They were our "second homes", where we gathered with our extended families and played cards and even celebrated milestone moments. Everyone would sit around the large table and share stories about past calls and razz each other about their less than stellar moments.

I would love to say I have all the answers, but one idea I do have is that if people invested even four (4) hours of their week to their community that they would otherwise spend on social media, we would have an incredible upswing of volunteers.

Volunteer opportunities are diverse and endless, from serving our veterans, to staffing hospice homes and animal shelters, to serving on your PTA, building homes, or responding to emergencies. All you need is an interest and a desire to make your community a little better than it was before you stepped up. Most organizations train you for your position. The hearts you touch, the teammates you work with, and the experiences you will have will leave an indelible mark on your life.

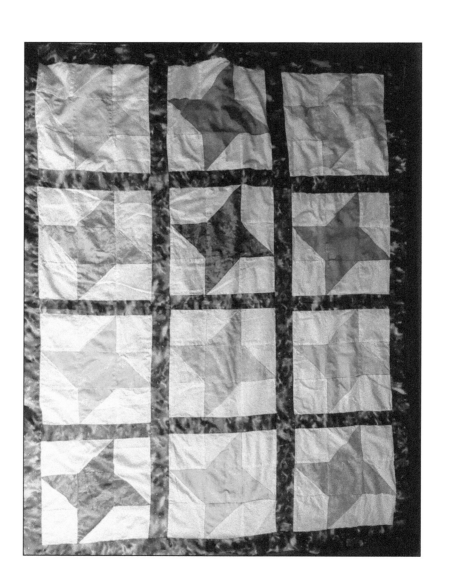

8

QUILTS

Quilts are messengers of the very best kind.
They deliver stories of history, art, and most of all, Love.

I HAVE BEEN sewing for over forty years and quilting for thirty. I was blessed to have learned to sew from both of my grandmas and my Aunt Elaine. I still enjoy spending time with my aunt as we tackle new sewing projects or just have a blast shopping for more fabric (which neither of us needs). We haven't been able to spend as much time together this year, so I make sure I keep in touch over the phone.

I taught myself to quilt watching quilting shows and poring over magazines and books, some of which I still have. I love fabric. I haven't met a quilter that doesn't. My favorites are batiks and prints that can be used for landscape quilts. Each fabric tells a story of what the artist was thinking and feeling at the time each design was made.

My goal in designing quilts is to create a bigger picture. I have made over forty quilts. Most of them have been gifts for family and my sons' elementary school teachers. I have also donated some to charities and sold others.

The quilts I made my husband and sons all had the same flannel, chamois, and denim fabric, which were positioned differently to identify which quilt belonged to who. Ben and Chris were two and four when I made them, so I will be needing to make new ones that cover more than their lower legs now that they are grown.

The ones given as gifts were each made according to a theme or pattern that came to mind when I thought about the recipient. My first family (parents and siblings) each received quilts with colors and patterns that I thought reflected their interests and personalities.

My sister used hers so much that the seams fell apart, so she gave it back to me to repair. The top is completed with double stitching for reinforcement, but I still need to finish it. I promise she will receive it before the end of 2021.

I am sure you must be thinking that my sister's quilt story is exactly why you have put yours away safe and sound. Please use your quilts! Whether they're hung up as a piece of art or used to keep you warm. Have them out so that friends and family can see and use them.

A quilt's story does not end when it is finished and given away. It is meant to continue creating and telling a history of its many years of wrapping you and your loved ones up during times of illness and storms when the power goes out. Don't worry about stains. You can find advice everywhere, including quilting stores, on how to get them out of fabric. If it doesn't come completely out, then it becomes part of the quilt's story. Think of the stains like the markings on a doorframe where your child's or grandchild's measurements are recorded. Each mark is now a new chapter in the quilt's story.

When I give quilts for kids, I expect them to be used and loved.). I also reinforce all my seams. When I spend weeks and months working on a quilt for someone, I want to know that it is being used, not put away for fear of something happening to it. I know other quilters feel the same way.

Show off your quilts! They could be an ice breaker that starts a conversation with guests. At the very least, it is a visual reminder every day of the love that went into making it just for you.

9

PHOTOGRAPHY

I have learned the most important lesson in photography, and that is: Remember to put your camera aside and fully experience all that is around you first.

THIS MEANS USING all your senses—smelling the fresh air, feeling the breeze as it whooshes past your face, and digging your bare feet into the grassy ground below. If you live in the city, it means taking in the aromas of your favorite restaurants or bakeries, feeling the energy of people on their way to somewhere, or admiring the storefronts on streets that you pass by every day.

Now, pick up your camera and snap away. You have now become part of your photos, and the connection you feel when you see them through the lens is that much stronger. Only then, I believe, can you fully capture with your camera what you have just experienced.

For years, I spent most of my adventures behind the camera. It was not uncommon for me to take over 500 pictures during a weeklong trip and then sort

29

and delete the less than desirable ones when I got home. I also managed to drop two cameras and break them both. Fortunately, they were not super expensive. I have learned to be more careful. In doing so, however, I feel that I wasn't really "focusing" on the journey but instead on keeping the camera safe. I have since learned to carry it in a padded case during my travels.

Wherever I go, I offer to take photos of other families, groups, and couples, and most times they are very pleased for the offer and with the results. I don't know about you, but so many times there is usually one family member missing from vacation photos. If I can change that one photo at a time, I am happy.

I have climbed both Rondaxe and Rocky Mountain in the Adirondacks numerous times over the last two decades. Each time is an experience, and the views at the top are breathtaking. I almost always brought my camera up with me, but now I am taking what I have learned and setting my camera down when I reach the top. The pictures will change from season to season, but the feeling each time I climb to the top is an accomplishment and something to celebrate and appreciate. From now on, I will sit back and embrace the beauty that surrounds me first.

All these experiences are gifts from God. I believe nature is one of His greatest gifts to us. We just need to invest in the time to slow down, take it all in, and thank Him for them.

10

PREFERRED SEATING

PEOPLE OFTEN THINK of preferred seating as having an unobstructed view during a performance. The truth is, preferred seating is wherever you are happiest while sitting. It could be a chair or couch that once belonged to a loved one that was passed down to you, or it could be that lounger you saved up for.

We all have our favorite places to sit in our homes. Most of them have the best view of the TV. Others are those comfy cozy chairs where we rock our kids to sleep or immerse ourselves in a good book. I have both, and they are in different rooms.

When it comes to outside, though, I look for those spots where I can look out onto the water or out on any of God's amazing creations. The photos you see in this section are ones that I could see myself in for hours; especially if I have good company. With all the rushing from place to place, it just feels good to "sit a spell."

I hope this inspires you to look at seating with a whole new perspective. It is not always just a place to rest, but also to take in everything around you and reflect on all that is going well in your life. If you happen to have a special someone, friend, or child to share it with, then all the better.

Consider it an investment in your mental health. Make that time spent the best it can be.

11

Injuries and Illnesses

INJURIES AND ILLNESSES are not things that we would wish upon ourselves or others. However, they do happen. It seems like accidents occurred for me much more often than others. I have often joked that I became an Emergency Medical Technician so I could take care of myself.

Whether our medical issues are major or minor, acute or chronic, we have to accept the current situation as it is and work with our medical professionals for the best possible outcome. Sometimes it feels like there is no positive outcome when it comes to some diseases or injuries, and we are left with only days or months to spend with our loved ones. I have lost friends and family, and know there is no sugar coating the pain that comes with loss.

As hard as it is to accept, we need to remember that we are here for a "season" and that we are to make the most of it. None of us knows what lies ahead, but if we live fully and enjoy the time spent together, we will all be richly blessed.

Our illnesses and medical challenges can be gifts if we allow them to be. They provide opportunities to build relationships where there may not have been before. These could be family relationships, for instance, that were previously strained or just not close.

My husband's parents lived in Alabama for a few years before my father-in-law passed. My mother-in-law moved back up to Rochester eventually. Shortly thereafter she was diagnosed with breast cancer, which she survived, and then shortly after that we discovered she had multiple sclerosis. It was during our visits to the doctors and procedures that we grew closer, and I believe we both grew to appreciate everything the other had to offer.

Illnesses and injuries can teach us to be more compassionate to others going through medical and/or emotional hardships. It is hard for anyone who has not walked in the footsteps of others to understand all of what they are dealing with. When I broke my ankle last year, Jacki took me to the mall and I needed a scooter. None were available, but they did have an extra-wide wheelchair for me until then. Have you ever tried to get through store aisles with shoes littering the pathway? How about smaller stores that have displays so close together that you need to be a size four to fit between?

In cases where an accident has laid us up, we must focus on what we can do, or, at the very least, what we can let others do for us. When we find ourselves or our families in medical crises (however big or small they may be), our friends and family often feel powerless, unsure of what they can do to help us. Sharing our needs gives them a sense of purpose. God puts it in their hearts to help us. Who are we to deny that gift?

Our medical circumstances may ignite a passion within us to start a new career in the medical field. We may discover a need that is not currently being met and create something new, whether it be cutting-edge technology or simply something that brightens the days of those stuck in hospitals and nursing homes.

Keep yourself open to all that is possible during this time and the things you will learn about yourself will help you as you progress through your days. Hopefully, you will arrive each new day with a better understanding of where you are headed in this journey called life.

12

SCARS

Some people may look at me and see my scars.
I look at myself and see that I am a living scrapbook of my experiences.

OUR SCARS MAY not be visible, but they are still there. Whether they are external or internal, they tell a story that is ours alone to share if we so choose.

Scars are proof that we are survivors of our experiences. Some we can put behind us and move on; others are daily reminders of events we have yet to come to terms with. I believe this is especially true for our veterans and first responders, as well as others who have suffered and survived traumatic experiences.

No matter how our scars became part of us, it is up to us to decide our futures. If we struggle with them, then it means we need to share them with a trusted contact who can help us through. That could be a friend, family member, doctor, or counselor. God is the best listener of all. And on that note: remember, that single set of footprints in the sand.

As long as we are still living, then I believe we still have purpose, whether that purpose is to carry out the mission or dream of someone who has passed, or to fulfill our own... even if we don't yet know what that is.

The scars we carry due to choices we make may sting, or they may make us smile and think, "Well, it seemed like a good idea at the time."

13

EPISODES OF ADVERSITY

EPISODES OF ADVERSITY *make us what we are. We have the power to choose to let them overpower us...*

Or we can view them as those life-defining moments when we rise to new heights and gain a new perspective that we couldn't have even imagined before.

Episodes of Adversity are temporary roadblocks which provide opportunities for us to tap into our inner strength and achieve that which was once perceived as unattainable.

Episodes of Adversity are those situations that we can look back, reflect upon in the knowledge that we overcame them, and smile about a job well done.

Debbie Haskins
July 24, 2019

14

THE ACHES AND PAINS
OF NEW ADVENTURES

HAVE YOU EVER seen or heard of someone doing something you had never contemplated before? For me it was Parkour. Parkour is a form of exercise characterized by movement from one obstacle to the next. I hadn't gone through an obstacle course in years, but I thought, "How hard can it be?" There was no running—just balance beams, parallel bars, and blocks to climb up and down on. There was about ten of us and I was the oldest female at fifty years old. I thought *this can't be so difficult*, and it wasn't... that evening. I was at the gym for an hour and was very proud of my accomplishment of being able to pull myself up over walls (short as they were) about seven times in all.

Fast-forward to the next day, when my shoulder was not cooperating. After a visit to the doctor, I discovered that I had injured my rotator cuff pulling myself up the walls. Fortunately, it only took about a dozen trips to the physical therapist to resolve the problem.

Now, you may wonder, "What was she thinking?" Well, I believe that if there is something out there that you are interested in doing, then there (normally) is no harm in trying. We only fail when we don't put ourselves out there. There is growth in each of us when we discover that we can do things that bring us joy. If it turns out that we are not able to, then we can rest knowing that we at least tried and can have a new appreciation for those who can do that activity well.

One of my favorite shows is *American Ninja Warrior*, and for years I had this fantasy that I could eventually lose my weight and become the oldest woman to conquered the course along with my sons. Of course, I have come to accept that I just don't have the extra drive that is required to achieve that. So, in the meantime I cheer on the competitors, contorting my body as I watch from the couch to "help" them through each obstacle.

Since my Parkour adventure three years ago, I have gone zip-lining along the Niagara Falls with my friend Laurie and it was a blast. I can't wait for more new experiences like that. I have some close friends my age who cannot physically do some of the things that I enjoy, and I believe that makes me want to put myself out there even more. My reflection is this: if you want to try something, don't let anyone tell you that you can't because of your age alone.

I have also come to the realization that I shouldn't go after goals just to prove I can do something. I need to discern whether it will be a goal that, when I achieve it, will be something that will allow me to enjoy "the fruits of my labor." We are here on this earth but once, and I want to make every day count!

15

Unexpected Table Guests

"Don't neglect to show hospitality, for by doing this some have welcomed angels as guests without knowing it." (Hebrews 13:2, ESV)

I WAS EATING lunch with my friend Becky at a small cafe that she frequented, where she knew the owner. I had gone back up to the counter to ask for some water and a gentleman, who I will call "Gabriel," brought it over. It turned out Gabriel was a friend of the owner and was just doing a kind deed. He then sat down at our table, slightly catching us by surprise.

Gabriel and Becky were talking about how the owner was doing, but the conversation gradually became more about him and his relationships with family and life experiences. Becky and I listened and shared in his conversation, but after about twenty minutes or so, she and I wanted to get back to our lunch and conversation. Gabriel did leave eventually, allowing us to get back to our lunch. Becky and I had been discussing our goals and dreams for our businesses.

Becky owns a spa, which is how I first met her several years ago. Right now, I am working on turning my photography hobby into a career, as well as developing a way to integrate that with my quilting. That lunch was the first time we got together, and we were both looking forward to that day.

I had been reading Debbie Macomber's book *God's Guest List* and I absolutely loved it. She reminds us that God's plans for us are so much greater than what we can even imagine, and that means that the people He brings into our lives are there for a purpose, though we won't always know what that is at the time.

Not all people are going to be positive, goal oriented, and compassionate mentors. Some are going to be, as Debbie states, "prickly." These people are meant to temper our patience and teach us to look under the "prickly" to understand what may have occurred in their lives to make them that way. Only then can we create the opportunity to show them the compassion they need.

Debbie also wrote that God doesn't always bring people into our lives— He also brings us into the lives of others. I believe God brought the three of us together on that day because Gabriel needed us, as compassionate Christians, to listen and show him that he mattered.

Looking back to that day, I hope that Gabriel received what he needed from us. I don't believe we spent as much time with him as he may have wanted, but I do hope it was enough.

16

Journey Awareness

I don't get lost.
I find new ways to get where I need to go.

I KNOW WHERE I am going and how to get there most of the time when I am driving. When I don't, I use a map. Sometimes I use a paper map and others I use my phone. There are still occasions where I am either so deep in thought or in conversation that I pass the street I am supposed to be turning down. I don't usually get upset or angry, as long as I am not on a time constraint, because I look at it as an opportunity to discover some place I would not have otherwise seen.

I know for myself (and, I believe, for most of my generation and before), that when our parents were driving, we knew every landmark between home and where we were headed. I looked forward to each one because I knew that meant we were that much closer to our destination, especially when we were headed to our grandparents' cottages in the Thousand Islands (in New York).

Mike & I travelled a lot with our sons from the time they were very young. Mostly we went to the Adirondacks, but also to Alabama where Mike's sister and her family lived. We also had driving vacations to Williamsburg, VA, and Washington DC. Ben and Chris slept for much of the time in the early years. As they grew older, looking out the window didn't hold the same interest as it did prior, so Mike and I regrettably gave in and let them use electronics to keep them occupied.

I'd like to think I would do it differently if I had the chance again. I just don't know if I'd have the energy and focus to keep on the journey and keep them interested and not restless (or arguing) in the backseat. Many young adults and teenagers do not know how to get from point A to point B without their phones.

It's not too late, though, for those parents who are courageous enough to travel with their kids without electronics. Think of the possible outcomes:

They discover a sign for an interesting attraction for everyone – make it a game for everyone in the car to look and then enjoy what was chosen.

They learn to appreciate all the nature and architecture that isn't found in their region.

They find a sign for a great little diner or restaurant just down the road that you didn't see.

Most importantly, it could save their lives and the lives of those around them.

As we all know, cell phones don't work everywhere, and if there is an emergency, they need to know where they are and how far they may have to walk to get help.

17

BLOOM WHERE YOU ARE PLANTED

MY HUSBAND MIKE and I were on one of our many road trips around New York. This particular day, we were in Lockport taking in the history and engineering marvels that took place to get boats to the next level of water in the Erie Canal. Among all the concrete surrounding this waterway was a single beautiful flower that had taken root and blossomed although there was absolutely no evidence of a support system to ensure its continued growth. Concrete surrounded that single flower completely.

In my poem "Episodes of Adversity," I include various situations where we feel like there is no way to move forward. This could be a physical location where we feel there is no opportunity for growth, or it could be an obstacle that just keeps defeating us.

Sometimes our location is the perceived block preventing us from moving forward. If I ever feel that way, I just have to remember that flower to understand that growth is possible anywhere. If the episodes are obstacles, such as challenges or tests that we somehow can't find a way past, we need to pause and ask ourselves "Why?" For some, it may just mean "digging deeper." For others it may require further preparation.

Why did God put that lone flower in that spot? I believe it was His message to me and everyone else who sees it that no matter where you are or what conditions you find yourself in, God has a plan. His plan is not just for us to grow up, but to succeed and inspire others in the process. I believe that God's plan for us is perfect. When we rush to achieve *our* plan, we may be acting before His preparations are yet in place for His plan for us. As a result, we experience delays or even a different outcome than we would if we were patient.

This is another example of beauty growing in unexpected places.
It adds a little pizazz to the old building, don't you think?

18

THE BIG PICTURE

Picture a photograph or painting of a landscape. Then understand that while all is not perfect within, each singular imperfect object fits together perfectly to give us the image that we see and delight in.

WHEN WE LOOK out at a landscape, we usually see it from a distance. What we don't see is what has happened within—as all the downed trees, flooding, fires, or other events that have forced the landscape to adapt and evolve into the vision that is before us now.

Now let us translate that to humans. All of us have had obstacles of varying degrees throughout our lives. It is our everlasting spirit, pushing us to overcome obstacles, that helps transform and develop us into who we are today. We are the sum of our experiences and how we have managed to learn from them. We have the choice whether to use them to build us up and create a life we can be proud of and strive for, or we can let our challenges defeat us and use them as an excuse not to try.

Almost all of us have met people whom we admire for any number of reasons. I admire those who have overcome incredible tragedies and obstacles. Some of those may have been through their own past actions and choices. Regardless of how such events are brought upon them, their spirit and sheer will guide them so they not only carry on but they *shine*, setting such an inspiring example that I can't help but think, "How do they do it?"

I say, let us each be our own Big Picture and demonstrate to others that we are all a work in progress, developing through our imperfections. Be that example for others to see and follow.

19

NATURE'S ARCHITECTURE

THIS PICTURE WAS taken in Sawyer Park in Greece, NY, not too long after a great wind storm resulted in damaged and downed trees all over Monroe County.

To me it paints a picture of hope. It is serene, almost as if the limbs were set intentionally to create it. At the time of the storm, it was anything but serene, as wildlife homes and habitats were damaged or demolished beyond repair and animals had to create new shelter. The fish in the creek also had to adjust to all this new foliage and the limbs that had fallen. Over time, a new equilibrium was created, along with new plantings, and before us lies an incredibly beautiful new landscape that we could not have even imagined before.

This is a great example for all of us. Despite our storms, we can find beauty afterwards. It takes time to reveal itself, and we can't possibly put our own timeline on it. The effect this particular storm had on Greece was many uprooted giant trees, which took over entire front yards and even impaled a neighbor's roof next door. It took weeks for all the trees to be cut down and left at the road for removal, and months before the roofs were repaired.

Storms do more than damage, though. They provide opportunities for friends and neighbors to reach out and help one another in times of need, whether that be offering the use of a generator or providing food to those who are helping clear roads, driveways, and other damaged property. Over time the results of storm damage can create a whole new landscape, whether it be through new plantings or the repurposing of downed trees into back-yard furniture.

We need to look at the storms in our lives to see how we can use what we have learned through our own experiences, as well as what we have learned from others, to start over and create a future that portrays us as the newer, stronger versions of who we are.

20

NEVER THE SAME PATH

I HAVE WALKED *the same path before, maybe once, maybe twice, or maybe even a hundred times. Each time it is different because of my experiences before, during, and after.*

Each step, each observation of nature, and each experience with wildlife or with those who accompany me creates a new memory and adds a dimension to who I am and who I will be at the end of that journey.

I take time to appreciate every opportunity to enjoy every path I am on.

It changes me forever in ways that I don't realize at that time or in that place, but I know that down the road I will look back on that experience and understand how I have grown because of it.

I savor the moments on that path and immerse myself in the surroundings and in those moments.

I long for time to stand still, for I will never have this time again; because the next time... I will be new again.

21

LEGACIES

WHEN I HEAR the word *legacy*, I think of what will be left to our families or communities in regards to personality traits, philanthropy, and service projects that will stand long after we pass.

Many people consider their children their legacy, which I would agree with in part, but while they may have inherited our traits, they deserve to build their own legacies and not feel the pressure to perpetuate ours. It is one thing for them to pursue the same interests, or even continue with the family business if that is their passion, but another to do so under pressure.

I personally want my legacy to be: friendship, volunteering, generosity, and a sense of adventure. I want to continue to set the example of these four traits for my sons and anyone around me until the day God brings me home. I believe the best legacy we can leave our family is a life lived well!

I strive to surround myself with friends who help me be a better version of myself. When we choose friends wisely, we often get so much more than we could ask for. I also make the time I spend with friends (whether on the phone or in person) intentional. I don't ever want anyone to feel that I would choose to be anywhere but with them then we are together. Our experiences and relationships grow to be absolutely, positively incredible and rewarding.

Volunteering is essential for any community to thrive, and I sincerely hope that I have set a good enough example for my sons. I am proud of both Ben and Chris as they offer to help family and my friends, and support me in my volunteer efforts.

Generosity goes hand in hand with volunteering because volunteering is characterized by our being generous with our time, talents, and treasures. This has been a large part of my faith life at Bethany Presbyterian Church. We have been so Blessed; I feel it is our responsibility to share our Blessings with others who have fallen on hard times.

I never want to lose my sense of adventure. There is so much to see and do, I just can't wait to get going. Mike and I enjoy our road trips around New York and beyond when we are traveling. It doesn't end there, though; Mike and I are planning to visit all 50 states, including all the National Parks and discover all that that there is to see.

I am looking forward to doing as much as I can for as long as I can.

To sum it all up, I find the more I do for others and the more adventure I have, the happier I am—so I am just going to keep it up and hope that others catch on.

I am always on the lookout for signs and situations
to add humor to my photography. Please enjoy!

I hope my stories lifted your spirits, gave you a chuckle or two, and inspired you to look for new opportunities to grow personally and invite others along the way.

Sincerely,
Debbie Haskins

BIBLIOGRAPHY

McComber, Debbie. 2010. "God's Guest List: Welcoming Those Who Influence Our Lives". New York. Pocket Books, A division of Simon & Schuster, Inc.